THE
VERY TALENTED

SILENT
E

PHONICS READ-ALOUDS

Title: The Very Talented Silent E
ISBN: 9798335277211
First Published in the United States of America, 2024

Contributors: Manns, Yvette, author; Blu, Ana K., illustrator

Summary: When E gets tired of being overworked in words, he decides to go on an adventure. With the help of a magician, he learns new tricks that help him stay silent yet still be a part of different words.

www.PhonicsReadAlouds.com

THE
VERY TALENTED
SILENT E

Written by: Yvette Manns
Illustrated by: Ana K. Blu

One late afternoon in June, the consonants and vowels met to create words. All the letters worked hard, but E worked the hardest of them all.

First, E built the word "echo" with C, H, and O. Next, B and D asked for E's help to make the word "bed." Finally, P and T asked for help building the word "pet."

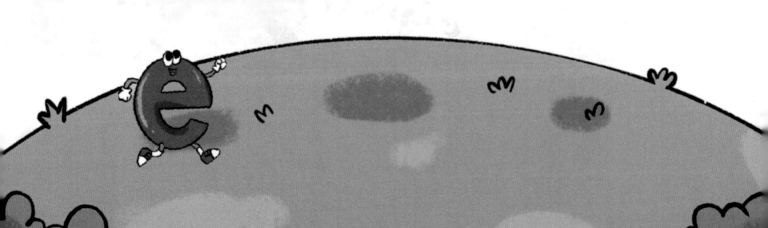

"Whew!" E exclaimed. "That was a lot of words! I need to take a break. Maybe you can build other words without me while I'm gone."

E didn't tell the other letters this, but he was getting a little tired from working so hard. "I need a change of pace," E whispered to himself.

E decided to take a walk. He left Vowel Valley, passed Consonant Cove, and ended up in the forest. "Finally! Some peace and quiet," E said, and breathed in deeply.

Sitting at the base of a pine tree, he noticed a cute white bunny hopping nearby. The bunny looked upset.

"Hey there, little bunny," E said with a smile. "Do you need help?"

She twitched her nose and gazed at E with wide eyes. "Yes, I do," she replied in a tiny voice. "I can't find my home, but I have a clue how to spot it. My house has a blue roof, and orange flowers are in front."

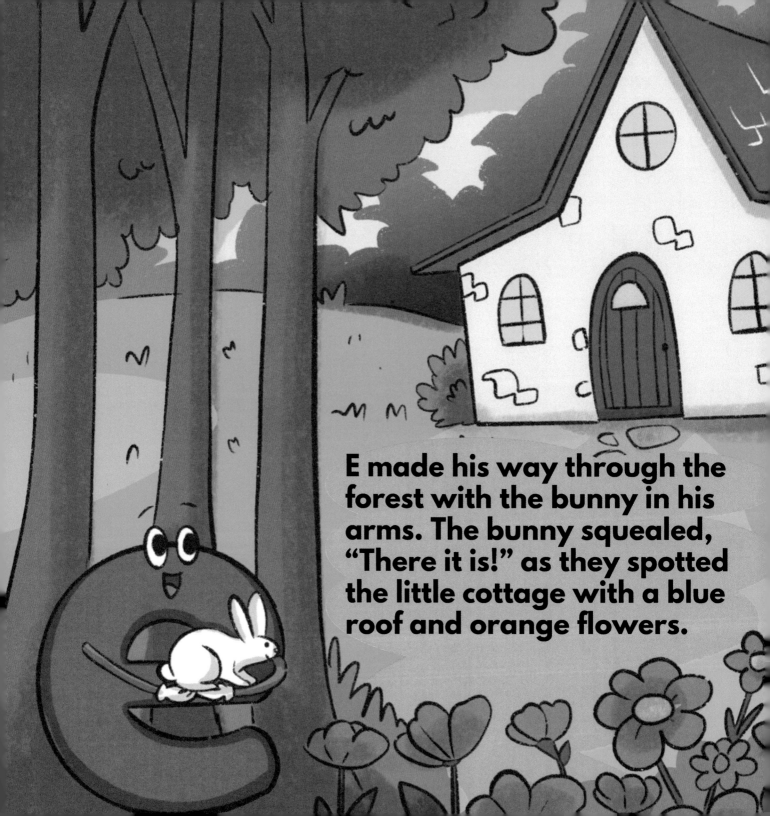

E made his way through the forest with the bunny in his arms. The bunny squealed, "There it is!" as they spotted the little cottage with a blue roof and orange flowers.

E rang the doorbell, and a polite man with a long beard opened the door. "Alice, there you are!" he exclaimed with a look of relief on his face.

E noticed the man was wearing a long blue cape and holding a wand.

"Are you a magician?" E asked.

"Indeed I am!" he replied. "My name is Luke the Legend!"

"Since you returned my bunny," Luke said, "I will use my magic skills to give you one wish." E explained, "I like the sounds my letter represents, but I wish I could be quiet sometimes. I use my sound in so many words!"

Luke responded, "Say no more!"
With a swirl of the wand, E changed from red to
gray and now wore a top hat, purple cape, and
white gloves. "Now, you can put your sounds
on mute whenever you want!" Luke said.

E exclaimed, "This is going to amaze the other letters. Can I invite them here for a magic show to share my new skill?"

Luke replied, "Of course! I'll teach you nine tricks you can perform to awe your friends."

At five o'clock, the consonants and vowels arrived at the cottage. E was backstage, and the letters sat in the audience.

A asked, "Where is E? I don't see him or hear any of his sounds anywhere."

Instantly, E appeared on stage. "Welcome, my friends. This evening, you will witness my magic tricks. I will amaze you as the sounds I represent become silent and change the way words are spelled and said."

"For my first trick, I will need a cap. Watch me change this cap into a cape by adding my Silent E. My first trick makes the vowel long in a word with a vowel, then a consonant, then Silent E."

"For my second trick, I'll need my friends I, U, J, and V. We know that English words don't end in your letters, but Silent E can help! E pulled out a white handkerchief, and it morphed into a dove."

I interrupted, "What about the words 'flu' and 'sushi'? Those words end in U and I."

E explained, "Some words we use are shortened versions of longer words. 'Flu' is short for 'influenza'. Other words, like 'sushi,' are borrowed from another language!"

"For my third trick, C and G can come to the stage. We know that C can represent the /k/ sound and G can represent the /g/ sound, but when Silent E follows them, C sounds like /s/ and G sounds like /j/. Now, we can build words like 'dance' and 'large'."

"For my fourth trick, I'll need my friend L. We know that every syllable must have a vowel. When the last syllable has a consonant, then L, then Silent E, we can build words like 'table' and 'puzzle'."

"Trick five involves my friend S. Usually, when S is added to the end of a word, that tells us that it is plural or represents more than one. My Silent E trick with S is that I can help you read words like 'mouse,' and you will know that it is singular, or only one."

"For my sixth trick, I will need two more volunteers, T and I. I will add Silent E to make small words like 'tie' look longer. Silent E can make short words appear larger."

"For trick seven, I can transform this cloth into a shirt for you to clothe yourself. When Silent E is after T and H, it makes /th/ represent its voiced sound."

"For my eighth trick, watch me magically transform these green 'goos' into a 'goose'. Silent E at the end of some words makes the meaning clear to understand."

"My final trick is my most mysterious trick of all."

"Sometimes, Silent E appears at the end of words and doesn't change anything. The words 'giraffe' and 'come' are examples of this!"

"These tricks that I learned will now be a part of my jobs when we build words."

"Thank you," E exclaimed and took a bow. The letters gave E a round of applause, and each threw a rose to him.

Luke declared, "Your magician name will now be 'The Magnificent Magic E.' Now go and explore your tricks with new words that have Silent E at the end."

The letters ran off to build the words "mice," "loose," "give," and "were."

mice   loose   give   were

A asked, "Does this mean E will be silent in every word we build?"

E replied, "No, I won't always be on mute. I will keep the sounds I represent whenever I am anywhere else in a word, just like in the words 'gem' and 'be'. Remember - our friend, Schwa, can also take my place in words like 'travel' and 'calendar'."

"Well, E," A said, "It was great learning about all your tricks. We can't wait to build words with Silent E at the end and practice your new jobs in words. How do you feel after a long day of performing?"

"QUITE NICE!"

E exclaimed.

TIPS FOR AFTER READING

- Go on a word hunt and list all the words in this story with Silent E.
- Sort the words you find by the jobs of Silent E and share them with a classmate.
- Read all the words with Silent E at the end out loud.
- Draw Silent E and explain the nine jobs in your own words.
- Using another passage or text, highlight all the words with Silent E that you can find.
- Find ten words that have an E, but the E is not silent.

FUN FACTS ABOUT
THE JOBS OF SILENT E

- Silent E has many jobs in words, which are listed as "tricks" in this book.
- Silent E makes /th/ go from unvoiced to voiced. An example of this is with the words "bath" and "bathe."
- Sometimes, words have a Silent E to keep the history of how they were spelled long ago.
- Silent E can do two jobs at once, such as in the word "dice." Silent E is making the vowel long and is making the C soft.
- Many English words are borrowed from other languages and may not follow the rules of Silent E. Examples: "forte," "karaoke," and "safari."
- Some people call Silent E Magic E, Final E, Sneaky E, Bossy E, Ninja E, Super E, and more! These are all ways to help us remember the jobs that Silent E does.
- Here are some more words that end in Silent E:

> are bathe done fable fine force give glue lake
> orange owe purse tease teeth turtle were

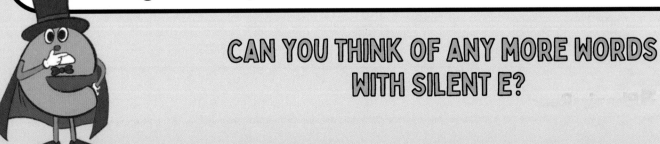

CAN YOU THINK OF ANY MORE WORDS WITH SILENT E?

CHECK OUT OTHER BOOKS IN THE SERIES!

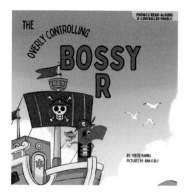

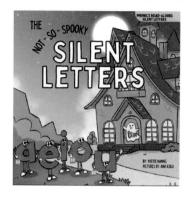

...and more books!

STAY IN THE KNOW!

Visit www.PhonicsReadAlouds.com for activities, stickers and more!

DID YOU ENJOY THIS STORY?

★★★★★

Please consider leaving us a review on Amazon. This helps us to learn what you want to read about next and tell other people about our stories!

 PhonicsReadAlouds    PhonicsReadAlouds   PhonicsReadAlouds

12598797R10019